God Has Not For— gotten

> *We must exchange whispers with God*
> *before shouts with the world.*

LYSA TERKEURST

PAIR YOUR
EXPERIENCE GUIDE
WITH THE
FIRST 5 MOBILE APP!

This Experience Guide is designed to accompany your study of Scripture in the First 5 mobile app. You can use it as a standalone study, or as an accompanying guide to the daily content within First 5.

First 5 is a free mobile app developed by Proverbs 31 Ministries to transform your daily time with God.

Go to the app store on your smartphone, download the First 5 app and create a free account!

WWW.FIRST5.ORG

MY DEAR FRIENDS,

I am so glad you are joining us as we study Ezekiel. This is an incredible book, and I believe an under-taught one. Some early rabbis would not even allow their students to read Ezekiel before the age of 30 — perhaps because it was too mystical, mysterious, explicit or graphic. And believe me, it is all of those things. Perhaps you've heard about the valley of dry bones or Ezekiel's vision of the Temple, but what about the many-faced cherubim pulling a chariot or when Ezekiel spent over a year lying on his side? This book is filled to the brim with amazing stories from a man who met with God intimately. The outcome of that intimacy is a book that puts the glory of God on full display.

The book of Ezekiel explores God's relationship with what the Bible calls a *"rebellious house"* (Ezekiel 2:5). This references the Israelites who seemed determined to abandon God. Instead of sending them away in anger, over and again God proclaims that *"they shall know that I am the LORD"* (Ezekiel 5:13). And my goodness, by the end of this book, there will be no second-guessing that God is Who He says He is.

God's glory is at the center of this book, and if you are anything like me, God's glory is a difficult subject to grapple with. His greatness is so far removed from my mundaneness that I cannot comprehend it — but I can try. By God's grace, He draws us near and reveals some of Himself to us. He sent His prophets to help us along the way.

So, come on in and explore Ezekiel with me. It will be a wild adventure, but if knowing God as the Lord is the outcome, this will be an adventure worth taking.

Camilla
First 5 Contributor

WHY EXPERIENCE EZEKIEL?

"AND I WILL PUT MY SPIRIT WITHIN YOU, AND YOU SHALL LIVE, AND I WILL PLACE YOU IN YOUR OWN LAND.
THEN YOU SHALL KNOW THAT I AM THE LORD; I HAVE SPOKEN, AND I WILL DO IT, DECLARES THE LORD."
EZEKIEL 37:14

All of the prophetic books share similar messages — God's judgment and restoration is coming — so why do we need so many of them? We need them for the same reason the Israelites did; we need reminding of who God is and what He is doing. And this, perhaps more than any other prophet, is so evident in Ezekiel. God is communicating not just His plans, but His character and love through Ezekiel.

"They shall know that I am the LORD" (Ezekiel 5:13). Through Ezekiel, God makes it clear that the Israelites don't really know Him. They are meant to be His covenant people, most dearly loved, but they reject Him over and over again. So they don't truly know Him, because if they did, they wouldn't continue to run from Him. If we are followers of Jesus, we become part of that same covenant people. What does that mean for us? We ought to take God at His Word, so when He promises destruction, be sure that it will come. (Ezekiel 7:3-4) When He promises wholeness, we can trust that it will be. (Ezekiel 16:62-63)

God uses Ezekiel to communicate that His justice — and therefore His punishment and judgment — is a necessary aspect of His holiness and righteousness. It is just as trustworthy as the rest of His character. Ezekiel does not try to address just one aspect of God's character and plan. He brings it all in because it is all God. By the end of the book of Ezekiel, we see a New Jerusalem and a New Temple. God doesn't leave His people in hopelessness. He presents Himself to them as Judge and Savior. (Deuteronomy 10:12-22; Ezekiel 12:37) His justice is good and lovely. (Ezekiel 16:62-63)

We need God's justice just as much as we need His love, and His justice and love came perfectly through Jesus Christ, His Son.

GETTING TO KNOW EZEKIEL

"AND AT THE END OF SEVEN DAYS, THE WORD OF THE LORD CAME TO ME: 'SON OF MAN, I HAVE MADE YOU A WATCHMAN FOR THE HOUSE OF ISRAEL. WHENEVER YOU HEAR A WORD FROM MY MOUTH, YOU SHALL GIVE THEM WARNING FROM ME.'" EZEKIEL 3:16-17

In 597 B.C., about 10,000 Israelites were taken captive to Babylon. (2 Kings 24:14) Among that group was a man named Ezekiel. (Ezekiel 1:1) He was a priest in his mid-twenties at the time of exile. He was the son of Buzi, who was also most likely a priest. He was taken when Jerusalem fell to Nebuchadnezzar, king of Babylon. Five years into his captivity (and at the same age his priestly ministry would officially start), Ezekiel received a call from God to prophesy. Now he was not only a priest but a prophet. (Ezekiel 2:1-3) God ordained Ezekiel as a watchman for His people in Babylon.

Ezekiel spent his childhood and priestly training in Jerusalem but spent his adulthood in Babylon prophesying primarily about Israel to the exiles. Ezekiel was a well-respected man among his people and was often consulted by the elders. (Ezekiel 8:1; 20:1) He was a contemporary of Jeremiah and Daniel, often prophesying about the same scenarios but from different perspectives and for different people.

Ezekiel had supernatural interactions with God which influenced the fervor and certainty with which he prophesied. Ezekiel's name is an apt description of his life: יְחֶזְקֵאל — meaning "God will strengthen." He had seen the greatness of God and was forever changed. (Ezekiel 3:12-15) God strengthened him and remained close to him throughout his life, creating a lasting ministry which influences us today.

Ezekiel was consistent with his message throughout his ministry, always pointing to the majesty and justice of God — His hatred of evil and His great love for His people.

CONNECT EZEKIEL WITH SCRIPTURE

"PHILIP FOUND NATHANAEL AND SAID TO HIM, 'WE HAVE FOUND HIM OF WHOM MOSES IN THE LAW AND ALSO THE PROPHETS WROTE, JESUS OF NAZARETH, THE SON OF JOSEPH.'" JOHN 1:45

The book of Ezekiel is dropped in the middle of an incredibly formative time in Israel's history. He is one of three major prophets that are active at this time who all had individual messages and audiences — Daniel, Jeremiah and Ezekiel. Obadiah also receives his prophecy during this time period. That God would use all of these prophets to speak during the same time shows us that He had a lot to communicate directly to Israel, Judah and all the surrounding nations. Ezekiel's message is distinct from his contemporaries though. He had a singular message tailored for the exiles in Babylon — God is making Himself known.

As modern readers of Ezekiel, we have the benefit of even more context. Not only does Ezekiel connect with many of his contemporaries by name and by similar details, (Ezekiel 8:1-18; 14:14; 28:2; Jeremiah 7:1-19) but the New Testament writers had a lot to say about him, especially in John's Revelation which beautifully corroborates Ezekiel 40-48. Ezekiel is best understood in the larger context of God's Word. If we isolate it from the rest of Scripture, our focus can narrow too much, and we'll only see parts of God. Since we are not the original audience, we have to be careful not to read only from our perspective and understanding but instead learn about the intent and reception of Ezekiel. This adds to our own personal perspective and understanding of the book.

So as we study through this text of Scripture, be on the lookout for references from other books. These illuminate Ezekiel and give us beautiful insights into the work and Word of God.

UNIQUELY EZEKIEL

"IN THE THIRTIETH YEAR, IN THE FOURTH MONTH, ON THE FIFTH DAY OF THE MONTH, AS I WAS AMONG THE EXILES BY THE CHEBAR CANAL, THE HEAVENS WERE OPENED, AND I SAW VISIONS OF GOD." EZEKIEL 1:1

There are a lot of things that make Ezekiel a unique book, but we will highlight just a few of them. The book of Ezekiel proceeds primarily chronologically. This may seem obvious, but much of Scripture (especially the Old Testament) does not read in the order that events took place. Instead, the Bible is grouped by type of writings — the books of law (Genesis-Deuteronomy), historical books (Joshua-Esther), wisdom literature (Job-Song of Songs) and prophecy (Isaiah-Malachi). But Ezekiel gives us a detailed timeline of what is happening around him, while also making incredible pronouncements. He even goes so far as to give us exact years! (Ezekiel 1:1, 2; 8:1; 20:1; 24:1, etc.) This allows for those who came after Ezekiel — including us — to verify his prophecy against history.

Not only is it chronological, but the book of Ezekiel is exclusively autobiographical. Many other prophetic works have evidence of being compiled by an editor. But not Ezekiel. The entire book is written in first-person prose which signifies a personal message that he handled himself. This autobiographical style is not necessarily superior or more desirable to editorial compilation — both are very appropriate aspects of Scripture, but Ezekiel's style gives us a consistent thread throughout.

Lastly, and perhaps most interestingly, Ezekiel encounters God in a wide variety of experiences and in a way that is not described elsewhere. Ezekiel sees across great distances, (Ezekiel 8:3) loses his ability to speak, (Ezekiel 3:22-27) enacts prophecies, (Ezekiel 4) falls to the ground in front of the great spirit of God, (Ezekiel 1:28) sees the cherubim, (Ezekiel 10:20-22) and visits Jerusalem in a vision (twice!). (Ezekiel 8:3; Ezekiel 40:1-4) None of these are unique in and of themselves, but to see them all in one person is incredibly unique. This speaks to Ezekiel's special nature in his role as God's priest and prophet to the exiles in this incredibly tumultuous time.

COMMUNITY AND CULTURE

"THEREFORE SAY, 'THUS SAYS THE LORD GOD: THOUGH I REMOVED THEM FAR OFF AMONG THE NATIONS, AND THOUGH I SCATTERED THEM AMONG THE COUNTRIES, YET I HAVE BEEN A SANCTUARY TO THEM FOR A WHILE IN THE COUNTRIES WHERE THEY HAVE GONE.'" EZEKIEL 11:16

The book of Ezekiel opens five years into the exile of the Israelites to Babylon. (Ezekiel 1:2) Jerusalem had been invaded and laid under siege, and 10,000 of its citizens were led out of the city as captives. The last date we get in Ezekiel is King Jehoiachin's twenty-seventh year. (Ezekiel 29:17) That means Ezekiel's prophetic ministry lasted at least 22 or 23 years. These years are some of the most desperate in Israel's history — their temple destroyed, removed from their home, taken captive and rebelling against their God.

Despite covenant promises, warnings and prophets, Israel continued to rebel against God. (Leviticus 26:14-45; Deuteronomy 28:15-68) The northern kingdom of Israel had already been torn apart, and now the remaining southern kingdom of Judah was facing the same fate.

Ezekiel was primarily speaking to the Israelites in Babylon, so his message is specialized for them in their local community and culture. (Ezekiel 2:3) Compared to Jerusalem, Babylon was enormous and incredibly impressive. It was a center of culture and politics, with its own religious structure.

The Israelites in Babylon needed a prophet, but what they wanted was immediate rescue. Many of the exiles in Babylon continued in the same sin that led to their exile in the first place. They worshipped false gods, sacrificed their children to them and completely conformed to the pagan life of the land. (Ezekiel 20:31-32)

Life as captives in Babylon for the Hebrew people likely wasn't as uncomfortable as we might imagine. There is evidence of open communication to those left in Jerusalem, religious freedom and access to commerce. Jeremiah had encouraged the exiles to live normal lives, and for the most part, they did. (Jeremiah 29:4-7) For the Israelites, this could have been a time of reflection, protection and return to God. Instead, it was an immersion into pagan culture, extending further into sin.

major moments of **EZEKIEL**

THE FOLLOWING IS A LIST OF SOME OF THE MAJOR MOMENTS IN THE BOOK OF EZEKIEL.
CHECK THE BOX AS YOU MEMORIZE EACH ONE.

☐ **EZEKIEL 1:**   Ezekiel receives a vision of the four living creatures and God's glory.

☐ **EZEKIEL 2:**   God calls Ezekiel to prophesy.

☐ **EZEKIEL 3:**   Ezekiel eats the scroll and is declared the watchman over Israel.

☐ **EZEKIEL 4:**   Ezekiel symbolically expresses the siege and famine of Jerusalem.

☐ **EZEKIEL 5:**   God's judgment is foretold through the cutting of Ezekiel's hair and beard.

☐ **EZEKIEL 6:**   The high places are condemned.

☐ **EZEKIEL 7:**   A final day of judgment is coming.

☐ **EZEKIEL 8:**   Ezekiel sees the abominations in the temple.

☐ **EZEKIEL 9:**   The unrepentant of Jerusalem are judged.

☐ **EZEKIEL 10:**   The glory of the Lord abandons the temple.

☐ **EZEKIEL 11:**   The glory of the Lord leaves Jerusalem but gives hope for a future reconciliation.

☐ **EZEKIEL 12:**   Ezekiel acts out the exile of Israel to a skeptical crowd.

☐ **EZEKIEL 13:**   The Lord gives an indictment of false prophets.

☐ **EZEKIEL 14:**   Elders visit Ezekiel but God sees their idolatrous hearts and God will judge Jerusalem.

☐ **EZEKIEL 15:**   Ezekiel relates the parable of Jerusalem as a useless vine.

☐ **EZEKIEL 16:**   The Lord narrates an allegory of His relationship with Israel.

☐ **EZEKIEL 17:**   God gives a parable of two eagles and a vine.

☐ **EZEKIEL 18:**   Each person is responsible for their own sin.

☐ **EZEKIEL 19:**   Ezekiel gives a lament for the princes of Israel.

☐ **EZEKIEL 20:**   The elders inquire of God again, and He presents Israel's history.

☐ **EZEKIEL 21:**   God has drawn His sword of judgment.

☐ **EZEKIEL 22:**   Israel violated their relationships with God and their fellow man.

☐ **EZEKIEL 23:**   The southern kingdom of Judah follows in the steps of the northern kingdom of Israel.

☐ **EZEKIEL 24:**   Jerusalem is falling, and Ezekiel's wife dies.

major moments of **EZEKIEL**

- ☐ **EZEKIEL 25:** Ezekiel prophesies against Ammon, Moab and Seir, Edom and Philistia.
- ☐ **EZEKIEL 26:** Ezekiel prophesies against Tyre.
- ☐ **EZEKIEL 27:** Ezekiel gives a lament for Tyre.
- ☐ **EZEKIEL 28:** Ezekiel prophesies against the leadership of Tyre and against Sidon.
- ☐ **EZEKIEL 29:** Ezekiel prophesies against Egypt.
- ☐ **EZEKIEL 30:** Ezekiel laments for Egypt and tells of their fall to Babylon.
- ☐ **EZEKIEL 31:** Egypt and its pharaoh will fall.
- ☐ **EZEKIEL 32:** Ezekiel laments Egypt and Pharaoh and describes their descent to Sheol.
- ☐ **EZEKIEL 33:** Ezekiel serves as Israel's watchman and receives message of Jerusalem's downfall.
- ☐ **EZEKIEL 34:** Ezekiel addresses the shepherds of Israel, and God sets His flock in safety.
- ☐ **EZEKIEL 35:** Ezekiel brings a prophecy to Mount Seir.
- ☐ **EZEKIEL 36:** God will redeem Israel for the sake of His holy name.
- ☐ **EZEKIEL 37:** Ezekiel experiences the valley of dry bones.
- ☐ **EZEKIEL 38:** Gog will come against the people of Israel.
- ☐ **EZEKIEL 39:** God will defeat Gog and all evil.
- ☐ **EZEKIEL 40:** Ezekiel has a vision of the outer temple.
- ☐ **EZEKIEL 41:** Ezekiel has a vision of the inner temple.
- ☐ **EZEKIEL 42:** Ezekiel has a vision of the temple chambers.
- ☐ **EZEKIEL 43:** Ezekiel has a vision of God's glory returning to the temple.
- ☐ **EZEKIEL 44:** Ezekiel describes the gate for the prince and the rules for the priests.
- ☐ **EZEKIEL 45:** Ezekiel sees the dedicated lands for God and the prince.
- ☐ **EZEKIEL 46:** Ezekiel hears from the Lord about the feasts and sacrifices.
- ☐ **EZEKIEL 47:** Fresh water flows out from the temple.
- ☐ **EZEKIEL 48:** The land is divided, and God resides among His people.

EZEKIEL 1

Write a verse that summarizes the reading:

Such was the appearance of the likeness of the glory of the Lord. And when I saw it, I fell on my face, & I heard the voice of one speaking.

MAJOR MOMENT: Ezekiel receives a vision of the four living creatures and God's glory.

Based on what you know from Scripture and the introductory reading, where does the book of Ezekiel pick up in Israel's history? Where does Ezekiel encounter God? (Ezekiel 1:2-3)

The Israelite's were being held captive in Babylon. In the land of the Chaldeans by the Chebar Canal.

Ezekiel described God as a stormy wind. (Ezekiel 1:4) Jeremiah, a contemporary of Ezekiel, described God as a whirlwind (Jeremiah 23:19; 25:32) What does a whirlwind usually indicate?

a tornado - a severe disruption of wind & force

The description of the four living creatures (Ezekiel 1:5-14) is astounding, and the interpretation of them is much debated. These interpretations are interesting, but perhaps not the most important aspect of these creatures. What is at the heart of these creatures? (Ezekiel 1:12, 20) What are the creatures bringing to Ezekiel? (Ezekiel 1:26-28)

The spirit of God - a message/the spirit of God.

What is the primary description that Ezekiel uses to describe the glory of the Lord? (Ezekiel 1:26-28)

appearance of brightness all around him.

In verse 28, there is an image of a rainbow that reminds us of Genesis 9. (Genesis 9:12-17) What foundation does this lay for Ezekiel and us?

It brings us to the promise & covenant that was made with Noah.

EZEKIEL 2

TODAY'S DATE:

Write a verse that summarizes the reading:

_____

_____

MAJOR MOMENT: God calls Ezekiel to prophesy.

Whenever someone comes close to the glory of the Lord, they have the same response. What is it? (Genesis 17:3; Joshua 5:14; Ezekiel 1:28; Daniel 8:17; Acts 9:4; Revelation 1:17) How does God often respond to this? (Ezekiel 2:1-2; Daniel 8:18; Acts 9:6)

_____

_____

_____

Ezekiel came into Babylon (land of the Chaldeans) as a priest, but was called to be a prophet. (Ezekiel 1:3; 2:3) Turn to page 14. How is the job of priest different than the job of prophet? How are they similar?

_____

_____

_____

What word does God use to describe Israel? (Ezekiel 2:5-8) How does God want Ezekiel to be different from Israel? (Ezekiel 2:8)

_____

_____

_____

What does rebellion look like to you?

_____

_____

_____

_____

EZEKIEL 3:1-15

Write a verse that summarizes the reading:

_____

_____

_____

MAJOR MOMENT: Ezekiel eats the scroll and is declared the watchman over Israel.

You may have heard Scripture referred to as bread or food — as nourishing as manna from heaven. (Exodus 16:14-18) Ezekiel 3:1-3 is a very explicit example of that. What does the Word as food mean to you?

_____

_____

_____

Despite the scroll being filled with _"words of lamentation and mourning and woe,"_ (Ezekiel 2:10) how did it taste to Ezekiel? (Ezekiel 3:3) What does this tell us about God's message? (Psalm 19:7-10; 119:103)

_____

_____

_____

How can God's message be bitter and sweet? (Revelation 10:9)

_____

_____

_____

Who is Ezekiel sent to? How does God say His Word will be received? Why does he need not be afraid of them? (Ezekiel 3:4-11)

_____

_____

_____

_____

The Priest and Prophet

Ezekiel served as a priest to the people but was also called to be a prophet for God. These might seem like interchangeable titles, but each has distinct roles. As we study Ezekiel, be on the lookout for how he fills both roles.

priest

Represents the people to God

Offers sacrifices and instruction on God's Word

An inherited position as a male member of the Levites

Organized and predictable training and duties

Law provided rules surrounding how the priests were to be honored and cared for

More removed and isolated from the rest of the community

Structured

prophet

Represents God to the people

Brings revival and a revelation from God

A calling by God

Charismatic and individualized styles depending on the prophet

No provision in the Law

Often a part of the community with other jobs

Spontaneous

EZEKIEL 3:16-27

Write a verse that summarizes the reading:

_____

_____

MAJOR MOMENT: Ezekiel eats the scroll and is declared the watchman over Israel.

What does it mean for Ezekiel to be the watchman for Israel? What is his responsibility? (Ezekiel 3:16-21)

_____

_____

_____

_____

Read Isaiah 21:6-9, Isaiah 56:10, Jeremiah 6:17, Hosea 9:8 and Habakkuk 2:1. A watchman was a common term used for a prophet — indicating their job as a lookout for danger.

What parts of the calling of the watchman do we also share? (Matthew 28:19-20; 2 Thessalonians 3:15)

_____

_____

_____

_____

As modern Christians, we have the benefit of the entire revealed Word of God. The ancient Israelites had some Scripture and also the Word from prophets. How does the Bible serve in similar ways as the prophets of the Old Testament? (Romans 7:7-14)

_____

_____

_____

_____

EZEKIEL 4

Write a verse that summarizes the reading:

_____

_____

MAJOR MOMENT: Ezekiel pantomimes the siege and famine of Jerusalem.

God uses different methods to communicate with His people. What method is He using in this chapter? Why did Ezekiel need this method? (Ezekiel 3:26)

_____

_____

Ezekiel was exactly where God wanted him, even though he was "impaired." (Ezekiel 4:4-8) He was used mightily by God. How does this correspond with 2 Corinthians 12:9? What weakness is God using in you?

_____

_____

_____

What message is God communicating to His people through Ezekiel in the first three verses? What does this symbolize? (Leviticus 26:17; 2 Kings 25:1; Isaiah 29:3; Ezekiel 4:1-3)

_____

_____

_____

Ezekiel 4:4-17 gives an even more brutal image of what happens to Jerusalem. What will happen in the coming siege?

_____

_____

Imagine watching someone live out future judgment before your eyes. How do you think you would respond?

_____

_____

_____

WEEK ONE NOTES

EZEKIEL 5

Write a verse that summarizes the reading:

_____

_____

MAJOR MOMENT: God's judgment is foretold through the cutting of Ezekiel's hair and beard.

This chapter is a continuation of the message being acted out. What is Ezekiel meant to do? (Ezekiel 5:1-4)

_____

_____

_____

Jerusalem was set at the center of the nations where God had chosen to dwell. (Psalm 48:2; Ezekiel 5:6) Despite all of that, how did the Israelites respond to God? (Ezekiel 5:6)

_____

_____

_____

Why is it important to know that Israel (symbolized by Jerusalem) did even more evil than the surrounding nations?

_____

_____

_____

Read Ezekiel 5:5-11. Why must God be against Jerusalem at this time? What does it say about Him?

_____

_____

_____

When God is satisfied it means that justice has been done. (Ezekiel 5:13) How does this passage make you feel about God's love of justice? What does His love of justice tell you about Him so far?

_____

_____

EZEKIEL 6

Write a verse that summarizes the reading:

_____

_____

MAJOR MOMENT: The high places are condemned.

A prophecy of condemnation for a mountain may seem odd, but these mountains had become defiled by pagan worship. The "high places" were literally altars set up high on hills and mountains. (1 Kings 14:23) What does God say He will do there? (Ezekiel 6:1-7)

_____

_____

_____

This passage echoes a big part of Leviticus 26:25-33. This warning had come before — many times over the centuries — but in God's great mercy, He is slow to anger. (Exodus 34:6) Through all of this, what is God's stated goal? (Ezekiel 6:7)

_____

_____

_____

God always promises to leave a remnant of His people, despite their turning their backs on Him. (Ezekiel 6:8-10) What is the future for the remnant? What would true repentance look like for them?

_____

_____

_____

God promises to destroy all of the evil abominations and idol worship. Why are these such evil offenses to God? (Deuteronomy 12:1-7)

_____

_____

_____

_____

EZEKIEL 7

Write a verse that summarizes the reading:

_____

_____

MAJOR MOMENT: A final day of judgment is coming.

Reading about God's wrath can be difficult for us, but why is it important for us as believers? What new insights about God did you find in Ezekiel?

_____

_____

_____

"The fear of God" is often used to describe the attitude we ought to have toward God. Sometimes it is referred to as "awe" or "reverence." Passages like this remind us that this is a fall-on-your-face-in-trembling recognition of how very high God is above us kind of fear (and love!). How can we know we are safe to draw near to God? (Proverbs 14:26-27; Hebrews 4:14-16)

_____

_____

_____

When the end comes, what will the Israelites realize has failed them? (Isaiah 2:20; Ezekiel 7:19) How had it become a stumbling block to them? (Ezekiel 7:20)

_____

_____

_____

Read Ezekiel 7:26. The people are seeking a new word from God but ignoring His law. What they needed to know was already in God's law, but perhaps they wanted an easier or quicker fix to their problem. When have you been tempted to look for outside advice or new words from God? What is the value in beginning with what God's Word already says?

_____

_____

_____

EZEKIEL 8

Write a verse that summarizes the reading:

_____

_____

MAJOR MOMENT: Ezekiel sees the abominations in the temple.

About a year after the vision in Ezekiel 1-3, Ezekiel receives another vision from God. What is he doing when this happens? (Ezekiel 8:1)

_____

_____

Ezekiel was physically in Babylon, but where did his vision take him? (Ezekiel 8:3)

_____

_____

_____

What is happening in the temple in Jerusalem? (Ezekiel 8:5-16) What are some of the laws that are being broken? (Exodus 20:4; Leviticus 11:44; Deuteronomy 4:15-18)

_____

_____

_____

God's temple was His chosen place to meet with His people. The place He created so that His people could come close to Him. What were the Israelites doing by defiling it?

_____

_____

_____

EZEKIEL 9

Write a verse that summarizes the reading:

_____

_____

MAJOR MOMENT: The unrepentant of Jerusalem are judged.

The vision continues with God calling seven angels (or heavenly beings). What are these seven angels there to do? (Ezekiel 9:1-2)

_____

_____

_____

The vision in Ezekiel 9 resembles a story from the past and the future. How does it compare with Passover and the tenth plague in Egypt? (Ezekiel 9:3-8; Exodus 12:12-13)

_____

_____

_____

How does it compare with the final judgment foretold in Revelation? (Revelation 7:1-3; 14:1)

_____

_____

No one in Jerusalem was without sin, just as none of us are without sin, but some were remorseful and repentant. (Ezekiel 9:4) Why is this significant? What is the function of repentance in your life? (Psalm 51:17; Isaiah 30:15; Joel 2:12-13; Matthew 4:17; Luke 24:46-47; Romans 2:1-5; 2 Timothy 2:25-26)

_____

_____

_____

How does it compare with the final judgment foretold in Revelation? (Revelation 7:1-3; 14:1)

_____

_____

WEEK 2 NOTES

EZEKIEL 10

Write a verse that summarizes the reading:

_____

_____

MAJOR MOMENT: The glory of the Lord abandons the temple.

The four living creatures from Ezekiel 1 are identified as cherubim. (Ezekiel 10:2) Cherubim often accompany the presence of God in the Old Testament. Where did images of cherubim reside in the temple? What was their purpose? (Exodus 25:18-22; 37:7-9)

_____

_____

_____

Where are the cherubim, the scribe, Ezekiel and the glory of the Lord all convening? (Ezekiel 10:3-4)

_____

_____

_____

How does the glory of the Lord appear at the temple? (Exodus 19:9; Leviticus 16:2; Ezekiel 10:3-4)

_____

_____

_____

Moses and Hosea each gave warnings about what is happening in Ezekiel's vision. What was it? (Deuteronomy 31:17; Hosea 9:12) Does it matter to you that the Israelites were warned many times? Why or why not?

_____

_____

_____

_____

EZEKIEL 11

Write a verse that summarizes the reading:

_____

_____

MAJOR MOMENT: The glory of the Lord leaves Jerusalem but gives hope for a future reconciliation.

The 25 men in Ezekiel 11:1 are likely the same ones from Ezekiel 8:16. They were worshipping the sun before, but what are they doing now? (Ezekiel 11:2)

_____

_____

God made His intentions known. The exiles in Babylon were right to leave Israel, and those that remained in Jerusalem were in the wrong. It was His city, but He planned destruction for it. Exile was bad, yes, but it was also the method of God's protection. (Jeremiah 29:1-23; Ezekiel 11:14-21) What were the false prophets telling the people who remained in Jerusalem?

_____

_____

God's plan of protection and reconciliation didn't look how the people expected it to so many of them rebelled and renounced God — incorrectly assuming He had abandoned them. Even Ezekiel was anxious and confused. (Ezekiel 11:13) What was God's actual plan for reconciliation with His people?

_____

_____

How do you respond when God's plan looks different than you expect (or hope for)?

_____

_____

_____

Recall an "exile" experience in your past where you now see God's faithfulness. Write it down and praise God for His good provision.

_____

_____

_____

EZEKIEL 12

Write a verse that summarizes the reading:

_____

_____

MAJOR MOMENT: Ezekiel acts out the exile of Israel to a skeptical crowd.

Read Ezekiel 12:2. Israel — the rebellious house — has all they need to see and hear God, but their rebellion keeps them away. What should be possible is impossible because of their rebellion. How can sin keep us from seeing and hearing God? (Matthew 13:13)

_____

_____

Despite their rebellion, God continues to use different methods to reach out and reveal Himself to the people. (Ezekiel 12:3) What method is He using this time? (Ezekiel 12:3-6)

_____

_____

We still have many methods to draw near and get to know God. What are some that you have experienced at church or on your own?

_____

_____

_____

Conventional wisdom of the time said that because the prophecies of judgment hadn't been fulfilled, they were all meaningless. (Ezekiel 12:22) How does God respond to this? (Ezekiel 12:23-25)

_____

_____

Isaiah and Jeremiah also faced this criticism. (Isaiah 5:19; Jeremiah 17:15; Ezekiel 12:22) The people didn't see immediate action, so they didn't take the Word of God personally. How can we stay spiritually sensitive to the Word of God, even when we may feel similarly?

_____

_____

Cherubim in Scripture

EZEKIEL TELLS OF HIS ENCOUNTERS WITH CHERUBIM IN THIS BOOK —
BUT WHAT EXACTLY ARE THEY? CHERUBIM ARE MYSTERIOUS
CREATURES THAT WE SEE A FEW TIMES IN SCRIPTURE, BUT USUALLY
WITHOUT A LOT OF EXPLANATION ABOUT THEIR ORIGIN. LET'S LOOK AT
SOME OF THE TIMES WE SEE THEM AND WHAT JOBS THEY SERVED.

GENESIS 3:24	Cherubim guard Eden and the tree of life
EXODUS 25:18–22	Carvings of cherubim cover the mercy seat on the ark of the covenant.
EXODUS 26:1	Cherubim are woven into the veil of the tabernacle. Likely the same image was woven into the veil that tore at Jesus's death. (Matthew 27:51; Mark 15:38; Luke 23:45)
EZEKIEL 1:4–28; 10:18–22; 2 SAMUEL 22:11	Cherubim accompany the presence of God, sometimes as His transportation.
REVELATION 4:6–11	The cherubim bring glory and honor and praise to God.

EZEKIEL 13

Write a verse that summarizes the reading:

_____

_____

MAJOR MOMENT: The Lord gives an indictment of false prophets.

Where are the false prophecies coming from? (Ezekiel 13:2, 17)

_____

_____

Putting words into the mouth of God is exceedingly dangerous and an affront to God's goodness. By misrepresenting God, the false prophets led others astray as well. What were the false prophets saying? (Ezekiel 13:10)

_____

_____

_____

It's possible that the false prophets believed they were speaking truthfully. But the reality is that their conventional wisdom and their human hearts were rebelling against the true Word of God. (Ezekiel 12:22; 13:2, 17) This can be a warning for us when something in God's Word feels wrong to us. (Jeremiah 17:9; Proverbs 3:5-6) What can we do when something seems wrong to us, but is scriptural?

_____

_____

_____

How can we know if we are speaking out of our own hearts or from Scripture?

_____

_____

_____

_____

EZEKIEL 14:1-11

Write a verse that summarizes the reading:

_____

_____

MAJOR MOMENT: Elders visit Ezekiel, but God sees their idolatrous hearts and will judge Jerusalem.

A group of elders comes to visit Ezekiel again but God sees into their hearts. What is interrupting their relationship with the prophet Ezekiel and with God? (Ezekiel 14:1-5)

_____

_____

_____

Read Ezekiel 14:5. This gives us such a sweet view of God's purpose. He desires His people's hearts. (Psalm 23:6; 1 John 4:17-19; Revelation 3:20) What are some ways God has pursued your heart?

_____

_____

_____

How have the idols created a stumbling block — a barrier — between God and His people? (Ezekiel 14:4-7) What would they need to do to be reunited to and not estranged from God? (Ezekiel 14:5-6)

_____

_____

_____

God hates their idols because He knows they are worthless and a waste. He wants what's best for His creation, and He is best. Why is following God best for His people? (Leviticus 26:12-13; Psalm 121) Why is it still best for us today? (Philippians 3:7-12)

_____

_____

_____

_____

WEEK 3 NOTES

EZEKIEL 14:12-23

Write a verse that summarizes the reading:

_____

_____

MAJOR MOMENT: Elders visit Ezekiel, but God sees their idolatrous hearts and will judge Jerusalem.

Ezekiel 14:14 tells us that not even the giants of Hebrew history could avert judgment on Jerusalem. Which men are named? What do you know about these men? (Genesis 6:9; Daniel 5:11-12; Job 1:1; 42:8)

_____

_____

_____

God makes it clear in this passage that judgment is individual. (Ezekiel 14:12-20) The people would not be able to rely on transferred righteousness. Each person is responsible for their own actions. Why is this an important aspect of God's justice?

_____

_____

_____

How can we know that there are still some righteous people living in Jerusalem? (Ezekiel 14:22-23) What does this mean for the judgment of the land?

_____

_____

_____

These few righteous would have been living in the middle of great opposition — still walking in the Way and doing good deeds. (Ezekiel 14:22) How can we remain righteous amid opposition? What is the purpose of this righteousness? (John 17:1-3; Galatians 2:20)

_____

_____

_____

EZEKIEL 15

Write a verse that summarizes the reading:

_____

_____

MAJOR MOMENT: Ezekiel gives the parable of Jerusalem as a useless vine.

In Ezekiel 15, the Word of the Lord comes in the form of a parable — a way of teaching using a story, often used by Jesus. What is Israel compared to? (Ezekiel 15:1-6)

_____

_____

The image of a vine is used a few times in Scripture, perhaps most notably in John 15:1-17. If Israel is the vine in the Old Testament (Genesis 49:11-12; Isaiah 5:1-7; Jeremiah 2:21), who is the vine in the New Testament?

_____

_____

_____

A vine that bears no fruit is a dead vine. How does this influence what happens to Israel and to those Jesus is speaking to? (Ezekiel 15:6-8; John 15:2-6; James 2:14-17)

_____

_____

_____

What is the only way for the people to be fruitful? (John 15:4, 9; Galatians 15:6-25)

_____

_____

Righteousness and fruitfulness can never be produced apart from God. Write a short prayer asking God to be near to you, allowing His Holy Spirit to fill you with His righteousness.

_____

_____

_____

EZEKIEL 16

TODAY'S DATE:

Write a verse that summarizes the reading:

_____

_____

MAJOR MOMENT: The Lord narrates an allegory of His relationship with Israel.

Ezekiel 16 serves as a sweeping poetic allegory, told in the first person by God. Before focusing too deeply on the details, what is the general sense the story gives you? How is it different than the way you usually feel reading Scripture?

_____

_____

_____

_____

Because allegories are not reality, it can be difficult to know which details to interpret literally and which to interpret figuratively. Read Ezekiel 16:30-31. Based on what we know about the book so far, how do you interpret this? What is literal and what is figurative?

_____

_____

_____

This passage is shockingly crude. How does that influence the way you read the story?

_____

_____

_____

_____

How will the Israelites see that the Lord is who He says He is? (Ezekiel 16:59-63)

_____

_____

_____

_____

And all the trees of the field
shall know that I am the LORD;
I bring low the high tree,
and make high the low tree,
dry up the green tree,
and make the dry tree flourish.
I am the LORD; I have spoken,
and I will do it.

Ezekiel 17:24

EZEKIEL 17

Write a verse that summarizes the reading:

_____

_____

MAJOR MOMENT: God gives a parable of two eagles and a vine.

Through Ezekiel, God uses an interesting parable to make Himself understood. This time it comes with an explanation. Using 2 Kings 24:15-17 as a guide, what are the specifics of the first eagle? (Ezekiel 17:11-14)

_____

_____

Zedekiah, along with Israel, rebelled against the provision God set up through Nebuchadnezzar. Who did they turn to in their fear? (2 Kings 24:20; Ezekiel 17:15)

_____

_____

The vine in the parable went from a strong, sturdy cedar to a low-lying willow. The willow is cared for and healthy, but it is humble. (Ezekiel 17:3-6, 14) Why do we rebel against humble circumstances? What is the value of humility?

_____

_____

No matter our earthly circumstances, we are no more or less in need of God. While Zedekiah looked to Pharaoh to help him, we are also prone to look to other people, routines or things to give us security. What is the danger of this?

_____

_____

Read Ezekiel 17:22-24. God has returned to using parable language. What image does He paint?

_____

_____

_____

EZEKIEL 18

Write a verse that summarizes the reading:

_____

_____

MAJOR MOMENT: Each person is responsible for their own sin.

Ezekiel opens with a word from God regarding a common proverb of the time. The proverb essentially says that the Israelites believed they were being punished because of their fathers' or forefathers' sins. (Ezekiel 18:2; Jeremiah 31:29-30) Why might they have assumed this? (Exodus 20:4-5) How can we know this is not true? (Deuteronomy 24:16)

_____

_____

_____

What is Exodus 20:4-5 actually saying about the impact of one generation's sin on the generations that follow?

_____

_____

_____

Ignoring personal guilt is a natural, human problem. (Genesis 3:12) How can we take responsibility for our own sin? Why is it a critical part of our relationship with God?

_____

_____

What do the people of Israel think is unjust? (Ezekiel 18:25-29) Is God's justice different than the way you view justice?

_____

_____

God hates wickedness but takes no pleasure in the death of the wicked person. (Ezekiel 18:23, 32) What is God's desire for us? (1 Timothy 2:3-4; 2 Peter 3:9; Revelation 22:17)

_____

_____

_____

WEEK 4 NOTES

EZEKIEL 19

Write a verse that summarizes the reading:

_____

_____

MAJOR MOMENT: Ezekiel gives a lament for the princes of Israel.

Ezekiel takes a drastic turn in literary form and gives a lamentation. Who is the lament for? (Ezekiel 19:1)

_____

_____

_____

The cub in verses 3-4 is Jehoahaz. What happened to him? (2 Kings 23:30-34)

_____

_____

What happens to the second young cub? (Ezekiel 19:5-9) Who does this refer to? (2 King 24:8-15)

_____

_____

_____

Read Ezekiel 19:10-14. What does this remind you of from what we have already studied?

_____

_____

_____

Many of the people of Israel were lamenting, but they were self-centered laments. How is this lament different? What does this teach us about mourning?

_____

_____

_____

EZEKIEL 20

Write a verse that summarizes the reading:

_____

_____

MAJOR MOMENT: The elders inquire of God again, and He presents Israel's history.

Recall Ezekiel 14. What happened the last time the elders came to Ezekiel to inquire of God? What did God require of them before He would answer? (Ezekiel 14:4-5)

_____

_____

This time the chance for repentance isn't offered. What does God have Ezekiel do instead? (Ezekiel 20:1-26) Why is God not allowing them to inquire of Him? (Ezekiel 20:27-32)

_____

_____

_____

Ezekiel 20:39 comes with a little bit of sarcasm. Essentially God is telling the Israelites to do whatever they want to, but don't drag His name into it. (2 Kings 23:4) Is this practice still a modern problem? How so?

_____

_____

_____

What does the future relationship between God and His people look like? (Ezekiel 20:40-44)

_____

_____

What is God's motivation for reconciliation? (Ezekiel 20:42, 44) How do we know we can trust that this is a good and holy motivation? (Deuteronomy 7:9; Romans 8:31-39; 1 John 4:7-8)

_____

_____

_____

EZEKIEL 21

Write a verse that summarizes the reading:

_____

_____

MAJOR MOMENT: God has drawn His sword of judgment.

Now Ezekiel is prophesying to Jerusalem and those who refused to be exiled. (Ezekiel 21:1-2) What does God tell him will come to Jerusalem? (Ezekiel 21:1-5) How is Ezekiel to respond to this? (Ezekiel 21:6-7)

_____

_____

_____

Who was to be the agent of the sword of God? (Ezekiel 21:18-22)

_____

_____

_____

What does God tell the prince of Israel to remove? (Ezekiel 21:25-27) When will they be restored? To whom will they be restored? (Zechariah 6:12-13; John 1:49; Revelation 17:14)

_____

_____

_____

God's covenant may be thought of as a primarily peaceful and merciful thing, but that is not necessarily the case. How is Ezekiel's prophecy in line with God's covenant? (Deuteronomy 28:15-68; Ezekiel 21:18-27)

_____

_____

_____

_____

EZEKIEL 22

Write a verse that summarizes the reading:

_____

_____

MAJOR MOMENT: Israel violated their relationship with God and fellow man.

Ezekiel outlines the two major categories of sin that Israel was committing — against their fellow man and against God. (Ezekiel 22:2-4) How does this correspond with what Jesus has to say in Matthew 22:36-40?

_____

_____

_____

_____

The Israelites have effectively committed every sin possible. It's troubling and painful, but there is great benefit in reading through it. (Ezekiel 22:1-31) What have you learned about the nature of sin through this chapter?

_____

_____

_____

_____

_____

How do you feel after reading through this laundry list of sin? Which sins elicited the strongest reactions? What does that tell you?

_____

_____

_____

_____

_____

EZEKIEL 23

Write a verse that summarizes the reading:

_____

_____

MAJOR MOMENT: The southern kingdom of Judah followed in the steps of the northern kingdom of Israel.

This chapter builds upon the imagery introduced in Ezekiel 16 with the two daughters representing Israel and Judah — the divided kingdom. (1 Kings 16:21-23; Ezekiel 23:1-4) Take a minute to write out what you know about the divided kingdom of Israel (and don't worry if this is the first time you are hearing about it!).

_____

_____

_____

During this time in Hebrew history, Israel is often referred to as the northern kingdom, while Judah is the southern kingdom. Samaria was part of the northern kingdom and Jerusalem was part of the southern kingdom. (Ezekiel 23:4) The northern kingdom of Israel was the first to fall into idolatry and "whoring." (Ezekiel 23:5-10) How would you expect the southern kingdom to respond after watching their sister nation fall? How did they respond? (Ezekiel 23:11-21)

_____

_____

After finding some semblance of comfort in Babylon (Chaldea) and Egypt, how would they repay Israel and Judah? (Ezekiel 23:22-31)

_____

_____

_____

The cup of God's wrath is a common image in Scripture. (Psalm 75:8; Jeremiah 25:15; Isaiah 51:17; Ezekiel 23:32; Revelation 14:10) This is the cup that has been removed from those who follow Jesus. How did Jesus approach this cup? (Matthew 26:39) How are we to approach it? (Matthew 26:26-28; 1 Corinthians 11:23-29)

_____

_____

_____

WEEK 5 NOTES

EZEKIEL 24

Write a verse that summarizes the reading:

_____

_____

MAJOR MOMENT: Jerusalem is falling, and Ezekiel's wife dies.

The Lord came to Ezekiel while he was a Babylonian exile to tell him something very important. What did He share? (Ezekiel 24:1-2) This is a pivotal time in the history of Israel. What other evidence do we have of this event? (2 Kings 25:1; Jeremiah 52:4) Why is it important that all three of the above Scriptures give us the same date?

_____

_____

In Ezekiel 24, we see Ezekiel using the same pot metaphor as he did in Ezekiel 11, but God gives him a slightly different interpretation this time. How does God end this interpretation? (Ezekiel 24:14) How does this compare with Romans 2:6-11?

_____

_____

In the midst of Ezekiel's work as a prophet, his wife dies. God called on Ezekiel in an incredibly trying time to be a sign for His people. How is Ezekiel told to respond? (Ezekiel 24:15-18) What reason is given that Ezekiel was not to mourn publicly? (Ezekiel 24:19-27)

_____

_____

Ezekiel's wife was his closest companion. In his prophecy, she represented Jerusalem and the temple to the Israelites. (Ezekiel 24:19-27) We aren't told exactly why Israel was told not to mourn when they completely lose Jerusalem, but from what we've studied, what might some of the reasons be? What evidence do you have?

_____

_____

Is there a time in your life when someone in the midst of tragedy has pointed you to God? How did the tragedy influence the power of the message?

_____

_____

_____

EZEKIEL 25

TODAY'S DATE:

Write a verse that summarizes the reading:

_____

_____

MAJOR MOMENT: Ezekiel prophesies against Ammon, Moab and Seir, Edom and Philistia.

Ezekiel prophesies against four other areas in this chapter. Fill in the chart below with the details of his prophecies.

SCRIPTURE PASSAGE	LOCATION	CRIME	PUNISHMENT
Ezekiel 25:1-7			
Ezekiel 25:8-11			
Ezekiel 25:12-14			
Ezekiel 25:15-17			

What connections can you make when reading these prophecies? What differences do you see?

_____

_____

_____

_____

EZEKIEL 26

Write a verse that summarizes the reading:

_____

_____

MAJOR MOMENT: Ezekiel prophesies against Tyre.

The Israelites were God's people. He chose them to fulfill His plan of revealing Himself to man, but that does not mean that He was only God to them. God is the God of the whole world, just as He was then. (Genesis 9:17; 2 Chronicles 20:6) Why is this important to remember as we read these judgments? (Psalm 96:10) Does this influence the way you read the passage?

_____

_____

_____

All of the foreign nations are judged for basically the same crime. What is it? (Ezekiel 25:3, 8, 12, 15; 26:2)

_____

_____

Jerusalem was being judged, but that did not make it ok to celebrate its punishment. How do we know what God feels about judgment? (Ezekiel 18:23) Why does the way we respond when others are punished matter? (Proverbs 24:17-18)

_____

_____

_____

God has — and will always — "set treachery to the deep" and bring beauty to the land of the living. (Ezekiel 26:19-20; 39:26-27) What kind of future does this bring to your mind?

_____

_____

_____

EZEKIEL ENGAGED IN MANY SYMBOLIC ACTIONS AS HE
BROUGHT GOD'S WORD TO THE EXILES. THESE ARE SOME
OF THE TIMES HE ACTED AS A LIVING PARABLE.

Ezekiel acts out the siege and —————— EZEKIEL 4:1-5:17
destruction of Jerusalem in three
ways: building a model with a
brick, laying on his sides and
burning and scattering his hair.

Ezekiel acts out the exile by —————— EZEKIEL 12:1-16
carrying his baggage around
with a covered face.

Ezekiel eats nervously, symbolizing —————— EZEKIEL 12:17-20
the desolation of Israel.

Ezekiel does not mourn his wife —————— EZEKIEL 24:15-27
as Israel does not mourn the
loss of the temple.

Ezekiel uses sticks to symbolize —————— EZEKIEL 37:15-28
the reunification of Israel.

ADAPTED FROM FAITHLIFE STUDY BIBLE

Symbolic Actions of Ezekiel

EZEKIEL 27

Write a verse that summarizes the reading:

_____

_____

MAJOR MOMENT: Ezekiel gives a lament for Tyre.

In the lament for Tyre, we are given an expansive (perhaps exaggerated) view of what Tyre was like. The exaggerations put an emphasis on what Tyre thought of themselves. What kind of place is Tyre? What is their primary source of glory or security? (Ezekiel 27:1-25) How did they see themselves?

_____

_____

_____

Tyre is first symbolized as a great and powerful ship. What is happening to this ship in Ezekiel 27:26-36?

_____

_____

_____

_____

Why is the pride of Tyre its greatest weakness? (Ezekiel 27:26-27)

_____

_____

_____

_____

Psalm 10:4 gives us such a perfect description of why pride is so powerful to disrupt our lives. When have you seen pride take up so much space that there was no room for God?

_____

_____

_____

_____

EZEKIEL 28

Write a verse that summarizes the reading:

_____

_____

MAJOR MOMENT: Ezekiel prophesies against the leadership of Tyre and against Sidon.

Ezekiel cuts right to the heart of pride in Ezekiel 28:1-2. What does it mean to *"make your heart like the heart of a god"*?

_____

_____

_____

The lament for the king of Tyre is overtly sarcastic and continues to make many references to the Garden of Eden. (Ezekiel 28:11-19) How does the story of Adam and Eve compare to this king? (Genesis 3)

_____

_____

_____

Like Adam and Eve, in an attempt to get closer to godhood, the king of Tyre moved further and further away from the one true God. (Ezekiel 28:6-10) What does God say is the way to be near to Him? (Hosea 6:6; Hebrews 10:19-22; James 4:6-8)

_____

_____

_____

After judgment comes communion with God. (Ezekiel 28:25-26) What shall the people know about God then?

_____

_____

_____

WEEK 6 NOTES

EZEKIEL 29

Write a verse that summarizes the reading:

_____

_____

MAJOR MOMENT: Ezekiel prophesies against Egypt.

Egypt and Israel had an especially contentious relationship and history. Despite that, how did Israel view Egypt? (1 Kings 10:28-29; Isaiah 30:1-3) Where would this lead Israel? (Isaiah 36:6; 2 Kings 18:21; Ezekiel 29:6-7)

_____

_____

_____

Ezekiel gives hope for Egypt, but what will be different? (Ezekiel 29:13-16)

_____

_____

_____

_____

King Nebuchadnezzar was the hand of judgment for nearly all of the nations Ezekiel prophesied against. What is part of his restoration for this difficult job? (Ezekiel 29:17-20)

_____

_____

_____

_____

The last verse gives us a glimpse of the future to come for Ezekiel. Who does the horn refer to? (Ezekiel 29:21; Psalm 18:2; Luke 1:68-69; Revelation 5:6)

_____

_____

_____

EZEKIEL 30

TODAY'S DATE:

Write a verse that summarizes the reading:

_____

_____

MAJOR MOMENT: Ezekiel laments for Egypt and tells of their fall to Babylon.

We aren't told how Ezekiel is feeling at this point after so many proclamations of judgment (and more to go), and it is unwise to cast our emotions on him, but imagine how you would feel if this was your prophetic career. Write a few sentences with what you might be experiencing.

_____

_____

_____

_____

What does this tell you about what you believe about God? About yourself? Does what you believe about God and yourself line up with what Scripture says? (Isaiah 53:4-5; Romans 8:37-39)

_____

_____

_____

_____

At the end of this prophecy for Egypt, we come to the same place — _"that they will know that I am the LORD"_ (Ezekiel 30:26). After studying over half of the book, why do you think it keeps circling back to this point? Has the meaning changed for you over the course of the book?

_____

_____

_____

_____

EZEKIEL 31

Write a verse that summarizes the reading:

_____

_____

MAJOR MOMENT: Egypt and its pharaoh will fall.

In his address to the pharaoh of Egypt, what does Ezekiel point to as an example? What allegory does he use? (Ezekiel 31:1-3)

_____

_____

_____

How is the tree described? (Ezekiel 31:3-7) Who is it attributed to? (Ezekiel 31:8-9)

_____

_____

_____

Assyria — and likewise, Egypt and its pharaoh — fell into an old and easy trap. What did they assume? (Ezekiel 31:10) What is the result of this assumption? (Ezekiel 31:10-18)

_____

_____

_____

What happens in your life when you attribute your strength to yourself and not God? What happens when you attribute it to God and not yourself?

_____

_____

_____

EZEKIEL 32

Write a verse that summarizes the reading:

_____

_____

MAJOR MOMENT: Ezekiel laments Egypt and Pharaoh and describes their descent to Sheol.

The Lord gives us a very interesting insight into the way that Pharaoh sees himself versus the reality of his influence. How does Pharaoh perceive himself? What is the reality? (Ezekiel 32:2)

_____

_____

_____

How will everyone react when observing God's wrath on Egypt? (Ezekiel 32:9-10) How do you react to reading about it?

_____

_____

_____

King Nebuchadnezzar was the hand of judgment for nearly all of the nations Ezekiel prophesied against. What is part of his restoration for this difficult job? (Ezekiel 29:17-20)

_____

_____

_____

Read Ezekiel 31:16-32. This is not meant to be taken as a literal description of Sheol. The theology of Sheol was not complete in the Old Testament and therefore can seem inconsistent — although it is not. Often "Sheol" was used as a placeholder for death or the underworld for the wicked and righteous. What do you imagine the purpose for this description is? What effect could it have had on the hearers?

_____

_____

_____

EZEKIEL 33

Write a verse that summarizes the reading:

_____

_____

MAJOR MOMENT: Ezekiel serves as Israel's watchman and receives a message of Jerusalem's downfall.

As Israel's watchman, Ezekiel is not held accountable for the Israelites' sin. What would Ezekiel's sin be? (Ezekiel 33:1-9)

_____

_____

The Lord is a life-giving God that finds no joy in death — even death of the wicked. (Ezekiel 33:10-11) How does He make this evident to the Israelites? (Ezekiel 33:12-16)

_____

_____

Human righteousness and wickedness are not permanent states. The relationship between righteousness and wickedness changed when Jesus gave His life. His life, death and resurrection covered the wickedness of all who follow Him permanently. As followers of Jesus, what is our relationship to repentance? (Luke 24:46-47; 2 Peter 3:9; Acts 3:17-26)

_____

_____

The Israelites left in Israel are clinging to a covenant that they have repeatedly broken. (Genesis 17:5-8; Ezekiel 33:23-29) What did the Israelites believe their worthiness to have the land was based on? What was the reality?

_____

_____

_____

God tells Ezekiel that he is essentially an entertainer for those who hear him and do nothing. (Ezekiel 33:30-33) Are we entertained or are we transformed by the Word of God?

_____

_____

_____

WEEK 7 NOTES

EZEKIEL 34

Write a verse that summarizes the reading:

_____

_____

MAJOR MOMENT: Ezekiel addresses the shepherds of Israel, and God sets His flock in safety.

The "shepherds of Israel" refer to the leaders of the nation — kings, princes, priests and prophets. (2 Samuel 5:2) What were the responsibilities of the shepherds? What had the shepherds been doing? (Ezekiel 34:1-6)

_____

_____

_____

The human leaders sought their own comfort and care while exploiting their flock, but our God steps in. (Ezekiel 34:7-16) God moves toward His people, seeking them out of their lost and scattered state. (Psalm 23) Reread Ezekiel 34:11-16. How does this passage enhance your view of God? How do you view your relationship with God?

_____

_____

_____

Next, Ezekiel turns his attention to the flock (Ezekiel 34:17-22) and addresses what we now call social justice. Some of the members of the flock were "_feeding on the good pasture_" while trampling the rest for others. How can we enjoy good things and support our neighbors?

_____

_____

_____

Read Ezekiel 34:25-31. Peace and safety are core desires for each of us, and God has promised a safe dwelling for His people. Through what means does God accomplish His peace? (Ezekiel 34:23-24) How does the pursuit of peace and safety influence your life?

_____

_____

_____

For thus

says the LORD God: Behold, I, I myself will search for my sheep and will seek them out. As a shepherd seeks out his flock when he is among his sheep that have been scattered, so will I seek out my sheep, and I will rescue them from all places where they have been scattered on a day of clouds and thick darkness.

EZEKIEL 34:11-12 (ESV)

EZEKIEL 35

TODAY'S DATE:

Write a verse that summarizes the reading:

_____

_____

MAJOR MOMENT: Ezekiel brings a prophecy to Mount Seir.

Moving into prophetic judgment after reading about how God takes care of His people can be a bit jarring, but the order of these passages may give us a better perspective on God's care. How does reading about the protective side of judgment change the way you read this chapter?

_____

_____

_____

_____

_____

Mount Seir is the name used for the area south of the Dead Sea where the Edomites lived. The Edomites were consistently hostile toward the Israelites. (Ezekiel 35:3) What do we know about their history? (Genesis 25:22-34)

_____

_____

_____

_____

God says _they shall know that I am the LORD_ in prophecies of protection and judgment (Ezekiel 34:30; 35:9, 15). How can we see God clearly in instances of protection and judgment?

_____

_____

_____

_____

_____

EZEKIEL 36

Write a verse that summarizes the reading:

_____

_____

MAJOR MOMENT: God will redeem Israel for the sake of His holy name.

The fate of the mountains of Israel are given in contrast to the mountains of Seir. (Ezekiel 36:1-15) How will God redeem His land? (Ezekiel 36:8-15)

_____

_____

_____

God has scattered His people out of His land, and in the process, the people profaned God's name. (Ezekiel 36:19-21) What is God going to accomplish by bringing His people back to His land? (Ezekiel 36:22-32)

_____

_____

_____

God gathered His people not because they changed in any particularly meaningful way, but because He has not changed. God is putting His holiness on display for Israel and all of the nations, consistent with His unchanging nature and holding true to His covenant. (Malachi 3:6) How does this relate to Romans 5:8?

_____

_____

_____

God's motives for salvation were of critical importance for the Israelites to understand, as well as for us. What did God want the Israelites to know about His motives for saving them? (Ezekiel 36:22-23, 32, 36) How does this knowledge create change in those that are saved? How does it change the way you think about being saved?

_____

_____

_____

_____

EZEKIEL 37

Write a verse that summarizes the reading:

_____

_____

MAJOR MOMENT: Ezekiel experiences the valley of dry bones.

By this point in Ezekiel's life, the Israelites had been in exile for at least 10 years. The exiles have effectively lost hope and are spiritually dead. How is this symbolized? (Ezekiel 37:11)

_____

_____

_____

Ezekiel sees the future recreation of the exiles, but it was not until they were reborn that they were truly brought to life. (Genesis 2:7; Ezekiel 37:8-10) How does God bring rebirth into the people? (Ezekiel 37:14)

_____

_____

_____

Israel and Judah (the northern and southern kingdoms) had been long separated at this point. How does Ezekiel symbolize their reunification? (Ezekiel 37:15-23)

_____

_____

_____

This sign-act symbolizes even more than the reunification of Israel; it indicates the coming of the Messiah — our Savior King. (Ezekiel 37:21-28) What will be God's ultimate declaration of who He is? (Ezekiel 37:28)

_____

_____

_____

_____

EZEKIEL 38

Write a verse that summarizes the reading:

_____

_____

MAJOR MOMENT: Gog will come against the people of Israel.

THE ORACLE OF JUDGMENT AGAINST GOG INTERRUPTS THE PROCLAMATION OF RESTORATION BUT THERE IS NO CONCLUSIVE CONSENSUS ON HOW OR WHERE GOG FITS INTO HISTORY. OUR BEST UNDERSTANDING IS THAT THIS IS AN APOCALYPTIC (OR END TIME) PROPHECY. THEREFORE, GOG WORKS AS A STAND-IN FOR A CHIEF PRINCE OF EVIL. (EZEKIEL 38:1-4; REVELATION 20:8)

As Gog comes against Israel, who is the instigating force? (Ezekiel 38:4, 16)

_____

_____

_____

At the time of Gog's attack, what is the state of Israel? (Ezekiel 38:10-12) How might this lead toward interpreting this as apocalyptic prophecy?

_____

_____

_____

God bringing Gog — an evil force — against His people may seem counter-intuitive, but what is the greater story happening? (Ezekiel 38:16, 23)

_____

_____

_____

WEEK 8 NOTES

EZEKIEL 39

Write a verse that summarizes the reading:

_____

_____

MAJOR MOMENT: God will defeat Gog and all evil.

God has moved from judgment to protection. What hand, if any, does Israel have in their own protection? (Ezekiel 39:1-8) What do they do after God has defeated Gog? (Ezekiel 39:9-16)

_____

_____

_____

Read Ezekiel 39:21-28. In what ways does God show His sovereignty to Israel?

_____

_____

_____

Colossians 1:15-17 shows us Christ's role in His Sovereignty — from creation to maintaining control over all. What does God's sovereignty mean to you in your life?

_____

_____

_____

In the end, after all is said and done, all shame will be forgotten. All sin and fear — gone. (Ezekiel 39:26) This is true of the eternal Kingdom of God, but as believers, we have the incredible opportunity to experience the Kingdom of God peek through on earth in moments of shamelessness and triumph over sin and fear. When do you see the Kingdom of God most clearly?

_____

_____

_____

_____

EZEKIEL 40

Write a verse that summarizes the reading:

_____

_____

MAJOR MOMENT: Ezekiel has a vision of the outer temple.

THE LAST FEW CHAPTERS OF EZEKIEL HAVE READ LIKE A THRILLING TALE. FROM NOW THROUGH THE REST OF THE BOOK, IT READS MORE LIKE STRAIGHTFORWARD BUILDING INSTRUCTIONS. IT CAN BE TEMPTING TO SKIM THROUGH THIS PART SINCE WE'VE ALREADY HAD THE BIG FINAL BATTLES, BUT LET'S STICK WITH IT BECAUSE THERE ARE SOME REMARKABLE DETAILS GIFTED TO US.

Where has God brought Ezekiel and what is He showing him? (Ezekiel 40:1-5) How does this compare to Ezekiel 8:1-6? About how many years have passed between the two visions?

_____

_____

_____

_____

Ezekiel gives us every measurement that we would need to recreate this perfect temple. (Ezekiel 40:5-42:20) What sense do you get of this temple from Ezekiel's detailed description?

_____

_____

_____

_____

Read Ezekiel 40:44-47. What do we learn about the sons of Zadok? How are they unique among the Israelites?

_____

_____

_____

_____

These are just a few

PROPHETIC BOOK	WHEN WAS THEIR PROPHETIC MINISTRY?	WHO WAS LISTENING TO THIS PROPHET?	WHAT WAS THE PRIMARY MESSAGE?
Isaiah	740-680 B.C.	People of Judah	God will judge His people and lead them to restoration after exile.
Jeremiah	627-585 B.C.	Jews in Judah and in exile	The people of Judah will be exiled to Babylon and Jerusalem will be destroyed.
Ezekiel	592-570 B.C.	The Jewish exiles in Babylon	Judgment follows sin and restoration follows judgment. All exposes the glory of God.
Daniel	605-536 B.C.	The Jewish exiles and gentile kings	Empires rise and fall, but God remains sovereign.
Hosea	755-725 B.C.	Israel (northern kingdom)	Despite Israel's unfaithfulness, God continues to be faithful.
Joel	620 B.C.	People of Judah	The judgmentjudgement of God will come like a locust plague, but first the Holy Spirit will come.
Amos	767-753 B.C.	Israel (northern kingdom)	Israel will be taken into captivity by Assyria because of their injustice.
Obadiah	586 B.C.	Edom	Judgment will come for Edom because of their oppression of Judah.

PROPHETIC BOOK	WHEN WAS THEIR PROPHETIC MINISTRY?	WHO WAS LISTENING TO THIS PROPHET?	WHAT WAS THE PRIMARY MESSAGE?
Micah	740-700 B.C.	Judah	Judgment will come for Judah because of their abandonment of God and moral decay.
Nahum	640 B.C.	Nineveh and Judah	Nineveh will not repent and will be judged. Judah repents and is saved.
Habakkuk	630 B.C.	Judah	Through conversation with God, Habakkuk learns about God's justice.
Zephaniah	630 B.C.	Judah	Zephaniah condemns Judah for their idolatry and warns of the coming day of the Lord. Even so, a remnant will remain.
Haggai	520-519 B.C.	Judah	Haggai calls for a rebuilding of the temple, bringing God back to the center of the nation.
Zechariah	520-518 B.C.	Judah	The temple must be rebuilt after the Babylonian captivity. The Messiah is coming!
Malachi	425 B.C.	Judah	The Lord deserves wholehearted devotion.
Jonah	790 B.C	Nineveh	Jonah brings warning to Nineveh, but God shows mercy on them.

EZEKIEL 41

Write a verse that summarizes the reading:

_____

_____

MAJOR MOMENT: Ezekiel has a vision of the inner temple.

While Ezekiel was on his tour, his guide went in and measured the inner room, but Ezekiel didn't follow him in. Why would Ezekiel have remained behind? (Ezekiel 41:3-4; Hebrews 9:7; Leviticus 16)

_____

_____

_____

Cherubim are carved into Ezekiel's temple vision as they were in Solomon's temple. (1 Kings 6:29-30; Ezekiel 41:18-20, 25) What was carved into the walls when Solomon's temple was defiled? (Ezekiel 8:10)

_____

_____

_____

What do you remember about the cherubim Ezekiel encountered earlier in the book? (Ezekiel 1; 10) What might this reencounter with the image of cherubim have reminded Ezekiel about the glory of God?

_____

_____

_____

_____

What significance do the cherubim have as depictions in the Lord's temple? (Exodus 25:18-22)

_____

_____

_____

_____

EZEKIEL 42

Write a verse that summarizes the reading:

_____

_____

MAJOR MOMENT: Ezekiel has a vision of the temple chambers.

One purpose of the temple was the separation of the holy and the common. (Ezekiel 42:13-14, 20) Why is this an important separation?

_____

_____

_____

_____

We still have sacred spaces and experiences in our lives today. How do you identify what is holy and what is common? What are some holy places in your life? What kinds of common things can creep into your holy spaces?

_____

_____

_____

_____

_____

Ezekiel was experiencing the promise of a restored and perfected temple. While we don't know definitively if this is a promise of a future physical temple restoration or of the perfect Kingdom of God (or both!) what do we learn about God through His promise?

_____

_____

_____

_____

_____

EZEKIEL 43

Write a verse that summarizes the reading:

_____

_____

MAJOR MOMENT: Ezekiel has a vision of God's glory returning to the temple.

What does Ezekiel experience now that he has toured the renewed temple? (Ezekiel 43:1-5) How does this contrast to the last time Ezekiel saw the temple in Ezekiel 10:3-19?

_____

_____

_____

It's hard to really imagine the magnitude of what Ezekiel was experiencing. What does the description of God's glory tell you about Him? What is God's plan for His temple and His people? (Ezekiel 43:1-12)

_____

_____

_____

What law does God give Ezekiel to distribute to His people? (Ezekiel 43:12)

_____

_____

_____

The temple was critically significant because it was the place of God's presence — the place where God came to accept sacrifices for the forgiveness of sins and to meet with the priests. Effectively, this was the hub of God's relationship with Israel. What does the insistence on its perfection tell you?

_____

_____

_____

_____

WEEK 9 NOTES

EZEKIEL 44

Write a verse that summarizes the reading:

_____

_____

MAJOR MOMENT: Ezekiel describes the gate for the prince and the rules for the priests.

In much the same way that the glory of the Lord came to Moses (Exodus 19:3-6), the glory of the Lord has come to Ezekiel. (Ezekiel 44:4-8) In regard to His law, how were these two men used by God nearly a millennium apart?

_____

_____

Through the Levitical Law, the Israelites — priestly and lay — had been given specific and holy jobs within the temple, but because they continuously outsourced these privileges, God took some of them away. (Leviticus 1-4; Ezekiel 44:6-14) Who were the only ones allowed to come near to God? (Ezekiel 44:15)

_____

_____

By giving away their God-given responsibilities, the Levites were effectively telling God that they didn't care to be close to Him. (Ezekiel 44:8) How would their punishment correspond with their sin? (Ezekiel 44:13)

_____

_____

Do you have any spiritual responsibilities that you are tempted to outsource or give away? What do you notice about times when you feel like giving these away?

_____

_____

The Levites had messed up their job, but God gave them the same promise that came from Moses — God is their inheritance. (Deuteronomy 18:1-4; Ezekiel 44:28-31) What does it mean that God would be their inheritance? What is our inheritance as followers of Christ? (John 10:27-28; Ephesians 1:3-14; Hebrews 9:15; Revelation 21:1-4)

_____

_____

EZEKIEL 45

Write a verse that summarizes the reading:

_____

_____

MAJOR MOMENT: Ezekiel sees the dedicated lands for God and the prince.

The exiled Israelites were likely (and understandably) preoccupied with their land inheritance. While Ezekiel addresses that, the more pressing idea he wants to bring is the purpose of the land — a place where God meets with His people. How does he do this in Ezekiel 45:1-6?

_____

_____

_____

The prince is then given his share of land and commanded to rule fairly. God's justice is not just cosmic, but domestic. This means that He doesn't only care about the overarching end story, but about the daily injustices as well. How does God expect Israel's princes to preserve justice? (Ezekiel 45:7-12)

_____

_____

_____

Another of the prince's duties is to be content with what God has given him. (Ezekiel 45:7-9) This seems obvious and straightforward, but we know from experience it can be incredibly difficult to achieve. How had the rulers of Israel demonstrated their discontent? (Ezekiel 45:7-9) Why is contentedness important? (Ecclesiastes 5:10; Hebrews 3:5-8)

_____

_____

_____

Again we see that in this vision, all are surrounding and servicing God as the center — now in the way of sacrifices and festivals. What will be the people's duty surrounding the sacrifices? What is the prince's duty? (Ezekiel 45:13-20)

_____

_____

_____

EZEKIEL 46

Write a verse that summarizes the reading:

_____

_____

MAJOR MOMENT: Ezekiel hears from the Lord about the feasts and sacrifices.

Read Ezekiel 46:13-15. Tucked in this chapter is this sacrifice that is described as "perpetual." Yet, this is not something we do as part of the Body of God. What took the place of this perpetual sacrifice? (John 1:29; Hebrews 10:12-14)

_____

_____

_____

_____

Ezekiel's vision does not necessarily serve as a command for the Israelites to follow. It stands separate from the law that was already given concerning the temple and sacrifices. However, it imagines a heightened experience — an age where the temple is grander and more controlled. The sacrifices are more frequent and exceedingly pure. Everything is simply perfect in Ezekiel's vision. If this is not meant to instruct the Israelites in new laws, what do you think is its purpose for Ezekiel's original hearers?

_____

_____

_____

_____

How can this passage encourage and instruct us today?

_____

_____

_____

_____

_____

EZEKIEL 47

Write a verse that summarizes the reading:

_____

_____

MAJOR MOMENT: Fresh water flows out from the temple.

Ezekiel's vision is centered around the temple, the place where God and man come together. In the same way that we no longer offer ritual sacrifices, as modern Christians, why do we not have a central temple? (John 2:18-22; Hebrews 1:1-2)

_____

_____

_____

In Ezekiel's vision, there is fresh, deep, life-giving water flowing from the temple. (Ezekiel 47:1-12) How does this water relate to the rest of Scripture? (John 4:10-14; 7:37-39; Revelation 22:17) How does the water flowing from the temple reinforce the truth of Christ as the temple?

_____

_____

_____

How does the water interact with all that surrounds it? (Ezekiel 47:7-12) How does this translate to us? (Galatians 5:22-23; 2 Corinthians 5:17)

_____

_____

_____

While making allotments for all of the tribes of Israel, God addresses foreigners who have come to join Israel and follow God. (Ezekiel 47:21-23) This is what we refer to as gentile inclusion. What does this tell you about the character of God and His will for all people? (Romans 9:24-29; 1 Corinthians 1:24; 1 John 5:12; Ephesians 3:4-6)

_____

_____

_____

EZEKIEL 48

Write a verse that summarizes the reading:

_____

_____

MAJOR MOMENT: The land is divided, and God resides among His people.

The allocation of land continues in what we might refer to as "theological geography." These land allotments are not literal physical boundaries, but designations of theological importance. These allotments are rich in history and indications of closeness to God. Who inherits the choicest land? What makes this the most desirable land? (Ezekiel 48:9-14)

_____

_____

_____

From beginning to end, Ezekiel has expressed the same message from God — He is making Himself known. In his vision of the perfected promised land, what is the capital city's name? (Ezekiel 48:35) How does this reflect Ezekiel's message?

_____

_____

_____

God is with us today, and yet we will be with Him more fully at the end of days. (Ezekiel 37:26-27; Revelation 21:1-8; 22:1-5) What does God's nearness mean to you today?

_____

_____

_____

Take a few minutes to write a prayer of thanksgiving to God. May His nearness be ever present in our lives.

_____

_____

_____

WEEK 10 NOTES

WHAT HAVE YOU LEARNED ABOUT GOD THROUGH THE STUDY OF EZEKIEL?

REFLECT ON EZEKIEL

"MY DWELLING PLACE SHALL BE WITH THEM, AND I WILL BE THEIR GOD, AND THEY SHALL BE MY PEOPLE."
EZEKIEL 37:27

At the end of Ezekiel, we can stand amazed at the incredible consistency of Scripture — the perfect story of God's love. God continues to choose His people, even when they do not choose Him in return. He does all things for the sake of His name. God doing things for the sake of His name need not scare us because His name is love and justice and mercy and holiness.

Through Ezekiel, God has revealed so much of Himself. We get the opportunity to see the Father, Son and Holy Spirit proudly on display. Not only that, but we are invited to participate. R.C. Sproul says in his commentary on John, "Christ is the temple, and all men are commanded to come to Him in order to worship and serve the one true God."

So let us come to the temple — our Lord Jesus Christ — and grow in the knowledge of our God.

She is clothed with strength and dignity;

she can laugh at the days to come.

PROVERBS 31:25

Proverbs 31 Ministries is a nondenominational, nonprofit Christian ministry that seeks to lead women into a personal relationship with Christ. With Proverbs 31:10-31 as a guide, Proverbs 31 Ministries reaches women in the middle of their busy days through free devotions, daily radio messages, speaking events, conferences, resources, online Bible studies and training in the call to write, speak and lead others.

We are real women offering real-life solutions to those striving to maintain life's balance, in spite of today's hectic pace and cultural pull away from godly principles.

Wherever a woman may be on her spiritual journey, Proverbs 31 Ministries exists to be a trusted friend who understands the challenges she faces and walks by her side, encouraging her as she walks toward the heart of God.

Visit us online today at proverbs31.org!

Proverbs 31
MINISTRIES